HEROIC ★ JOBS

RESCUE AT SEA

Chris Oxlade

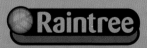

Raintree

Chicago, Illinois

www.capstonepub.com
Visit our website to find out more information about Heinemann-Raintree books.

To order:
☎ Phone 888-454-2279
💻 Visit www.capstonepub.com to browse our catalog and order online.

© 2012 Heinemann Library
an imprint of Capstone Global Library, LLC
Chicago, Illinois

Edited by Dan Nunn, Rebecca Rissman, and Catherine Veitch
Designed by Joanne Malivoire
Picture research by Elizabeth Alexander
Originated by Capstone Global Library
Printed and bound in China by CTPS

15 14 13 12 11
10 9 8 7 6 5 4 3 2 1

Library of Congress Cataloging-in-Publication Data
Oxlade, Chris.
  Rescue at sea / Chris Oxlade.
    p. cm.—(Heroic jobs)
  Includes bibliographical references and index.
  ISBN 978-1-4109-4360-6 (hbk.)—ISBN 978-1-4109-4367-5 (pbk.) 1. Lifesaving—Juvenile literature. 2. Search and rescue operations—Juvenile literature. 3. Rescue work—Juvenile literature. I. Title.
  VK1445.O96 2012
  363.12'381—dc22   2011015760

Acknowledgments
We would like to thank the following for permission to reproduce photographs: Alamy pp. 4 (© Tim Woodcock), 6 (© Jack Sullivan), 9 (© Tim Jones), 10 (© Simon Price), 13 (© stephen How), 19 (© WaterFrame), 25 (© Mike Greenslade); Corbis pp. 17 (© Andrew Fox), 18 (© Ton Koene/ZUMA Press), 27 (© Andrew Watson/JAI); Getty Images pp. 5 (Peter Macdiarmid), 8 (Hannah Johnston), 11 (Jeff J Mitchell), 14 (Spencer Platt), 15 (Matt Cardy), 21 (Matt Cardy), 22 (Johnson Liu/AFP), 24 (Ed Taylor); iStockphoto p. 12 (© Eric Gevaert); Shutterstock pp. 7 (© Jerry-Rainey), 29 top (© Warren Chan), 29 bottom (© Ruth Black); U.S. Coast Guard pp. 16 (Petty Officer 3rd Class Erik Swanson), 20 (Petty Officer 3rd Class Jon-Paul Rios), 23 (Petty Officer 1st Class David Mosley), 26 (Petty Officer 3rd Class George Degener).

Cover photograph of a Royal National Lifeboat Institute crew on the water at Porthcawl, Wales reproduced with permission of Corbis (© Andrew Fox).

Every effort has been made to contact copyright holders of any material reproduced in this book. Any omissions will be rectified in subsequent printings if notice is given to the publisher.

We would like to thank Paul Rhynard for his invaluable help in the preparation of this book.

Disclaimer
All the Internet addresses (URLs) given in this book were valid at the time of going to press. However, due to the dynamic nature of the Internet, some addresses may have changed, or sites may have changed or ceased to exist since publication. While the author and Publishers regret any inconvenience this may cause readers, no responsibility for any such changes can be accepted by either the author or the Publishers.

Some words are shown in bold, **like this**. You can find out what they mean by looking in the glossary.

Contents

Emergency!

At sea the wind is howling. The waves are as high as a house. A fishing boat is being tossed up and down. Its engine has broken down, and there is a sick fisherman on board. It's time for rescuers to take to the sea and the air.

Who Needs Help?

Ship's **crews**, passengers, sailors, oil-rig workers, divers, surfers, and swimmers all work and play at sea. Sometimes they get lost at sea. Sometimes they get sick or injured. Sometimes their ships and boats break down or sink. Then they need to be rescued.

Did you know? A cruise ship has rescue boats with enough room for everyone on board.

7

Rescuers work on rescue boats and on the beach. A small rescue boat has a **crew** of two or three. A large rescue boat has a crew of ten or more. Everyone has a job to do. The person in charge is called the **coxswain**.

Lifeguards are rescuers who work at the beach.

Air Crews

The Navy, Air Force, and Coast Guard have search-and-rescue helicopters. Pilots fly the helicopters. They are very skilled at flying. During a sea rescue they **hover** the helicopter over a ship, even in fierce winds.

11

Dangers of the Job

Rescuers in rescue boats and helicopters face super-strong winds, enormous waves, and sometimes very cold water. Rescue boats and rescue swimmers sometimes smash into ships and boats that are rolling back and forth in the big waves.

Did you know?
In the world's oceans, strong winds can make waves that are more than 100 feet high. That's as high as a ten-story building!

Coastal Dangers

lifeguard

Rescuers who work on or near the shore face extra dangers. Strong currents can pull lifeguards and other rescuers along the shore or out to sea. Helicopter **crews** are also at risk when they fly close to cliffs in strong winds.

Lifeguards often battle through **surf** to make a rescue.

Rescue Boats

Rescuers use different sorts of rescue boats. Big rescue boats can travel far out to sea in very bad weather. Their powerful engines push them along at high speeds. Small, high-speed rescue boats are used for rescues close to shore.

Did you know?
When big rescue boats get knocked over by a wave, some can flip back up the right way. This is called self-righting.

Rescuers carry lots of equipment in their boats and helicopters. They take **first aid** equipment to treat injured or sick people. They take stretchers to carry people to safety. Rescue swimmers carry radios.

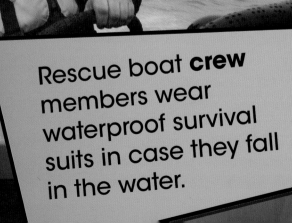

Rescue boat **crew** members wear waterproof survival suits in case they fall in the water.

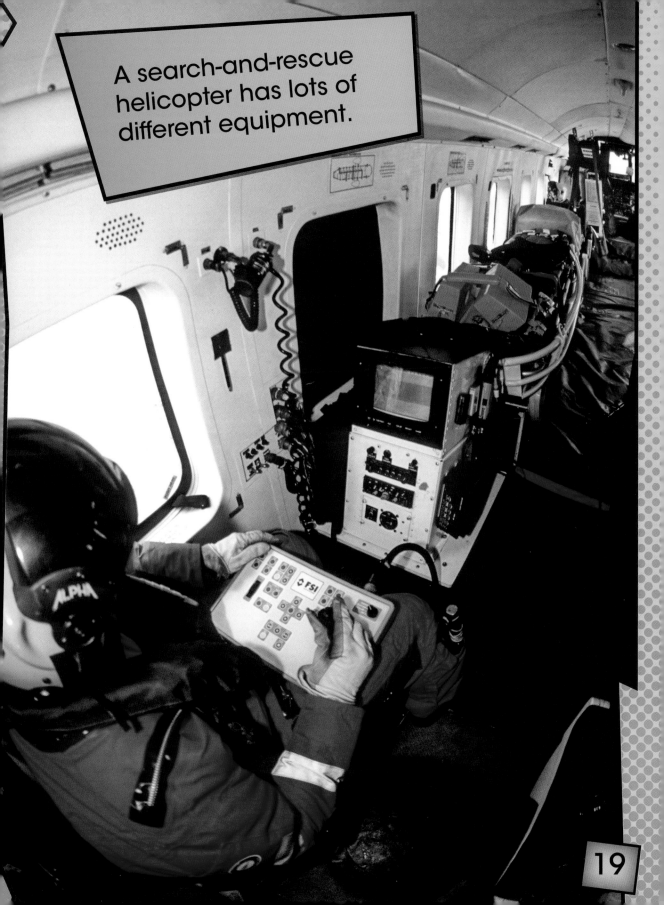

A search-and-rescue helicopter has lots of different equipment.

19

To the Rescue!

Mariners who get into trouble call for help by radio, or by telephone. They might also let off a bright **flare**, like a firework. It is important to tell the rescue team the following information:

- where they are
- what trouble they are in
- a description of their boat
- how many people are on board

The **crew** quickly launches the rescue boat and heads out to sea.

Helicopter Rescues

A helicopter **crew** is called into action if an emergency happens in a place that a rescue boat can't reach. It helps to search for small boats and people in the sea. Helicopters also take injured or sick people to a hospital.

Did you know?
Long-range search aircraft look for people who are lost very far out at sea, where helicopters and boats can't go.

Beach Rescue!

Many heroic rescues take place in the sea close to beaches. If somebody gets into trouble, other boaters, surfers, or swimmers raise the alarm. Beach lifeguards rush into the water to help. They pull the person back to the beach, and give **first aid**.

This lifeguard is rushing to the rescue on a jet ski.

Becoming a Rescuer

Rescuers need many different skills. Members of rescue boat **crews** must have experience in going to sea. Beach lifeguards must be strong swimmers and have good **first aid** skills. Helicopter crews need the most training.

These men are training to put out a fire.

In Australia, children can join the junior lifeguards to learn about the job.

Staying Safe at Sea

Many emergencies at sea and at the beach can be avoided by following some simple rules:

- Never swim in the sea alone.

- Always take notice of warning signs.

- Be aware of the tide.

- Always wear a **flotation device**, like a life jacket, when boating.

- If there is an emergency, tell a lifeguard, or call 911. Never go to the rescue yourself.

Did you know?
There are different emergency telephone numbers in the world:
- United States: 911
- Australia: 000
- most of Europe: 112
- UK: 999

DANGER
NO SWIMMING

Glossary

coxswain person who is in charge of the crew of a ship or boat

crew group of people who work on a ship or boat

first aid help given to an injured or sick person before they are taken to a hospital

flare item that produces a very bright flame. It is used as a signal for help by people at sea who are in trouble.

flotation device lifejacket or buoyancy aid that stops you from sinking in the water

mariner person who travels at sea, such as a yacht sailor or a fisherman

surf line of foam made by waves crashing against the shore

winch machine that winds in or lets out wire. It can be used to lift people in and out of a helicopter.

Find Out More

Books

Braulick, Carrie A. *The U.S. Coast Guard*. Mankato, Minn.: Capstone Press, 2008.

Doeden, Matt. *The U.S. Navy*. Mankato, Minn.: Capstone Press, 2005.

Hamilton, John. *The Coast Guard*. Edina, Minn.: Abdo, 2007.

Websites

www.sls.com.au/nippers/kids-zone
This is the website of the Australian Lifeguard Service.

www.uscg.mil/history/sarindex.asp
This part of the website of the U.S. Coast Guard has lots of information about search and rescue missions.

Index